PENNSYLVANIA

Love to you both
always,

Wendy and Dennis
1980

i

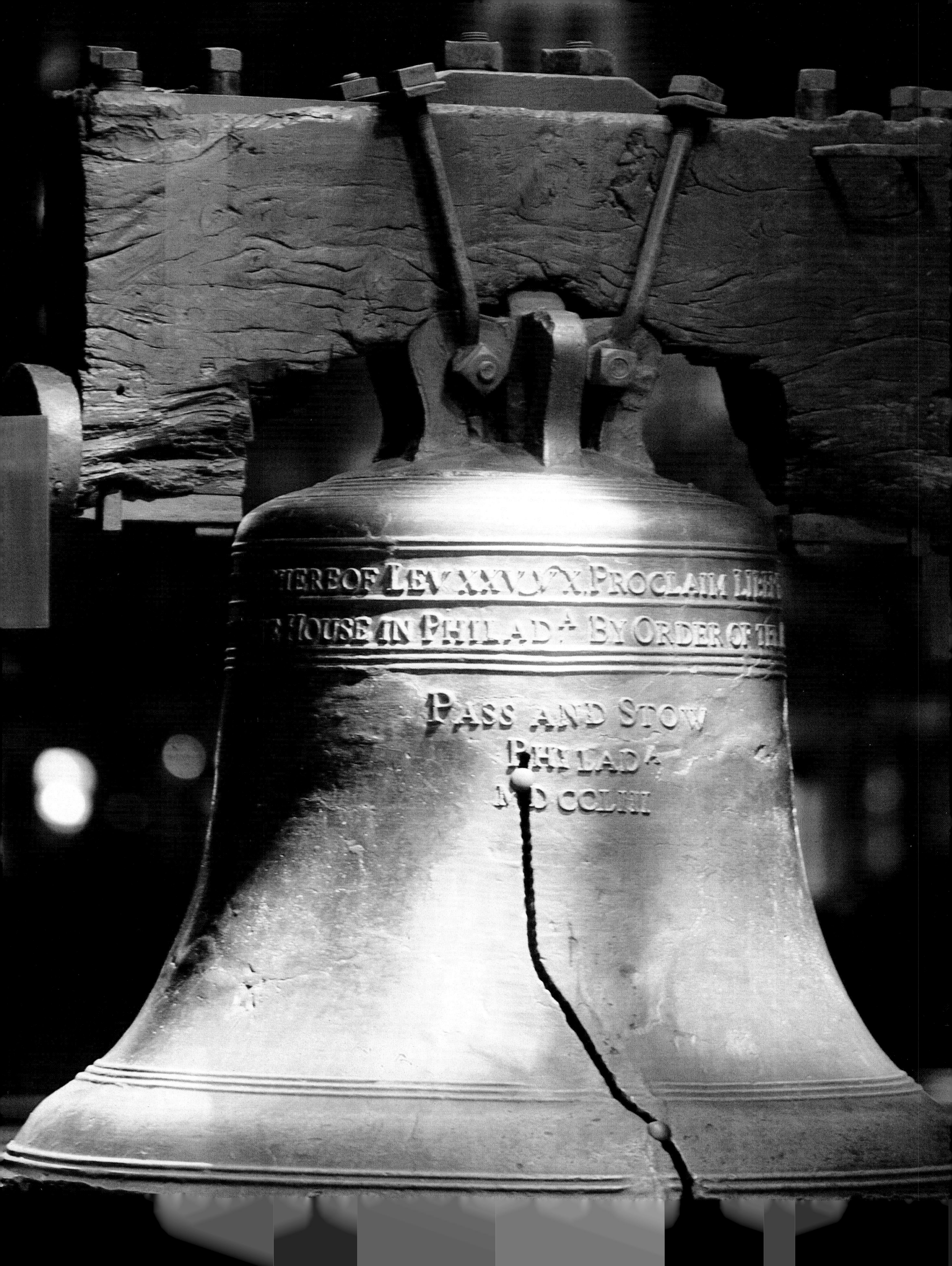
PASS AND STOW

PENNSYLVANIA

PHOTOGRAPHY • CLYDE SMITH
TEXT • CRONAN MINTON

Thousands come from all
over the world to see and
touch Pennsylvania's
incomparable Liberty Bell,
hanging in Independence
Hall. It is shown here
in a night setting.

International Standard Book Number 0-912856-40-8
Library of Congress Catalog Number 78-51218
Copyright© 1978 by Graphic Arts Center Publishing Co.
2000 N.W. Wilson • Portland, Oregon 97209 • 503/224-7777
Publisher • Charles H. Belding
Designer • Robert Reynolds
Printer • Graphic Arts Center
Binding • Lincoln & Allen
Printed in the United States of America

Spectacular aerial view of farmland overlooking Pennsylvania's Grand Canyon near Wellsboro.

"Fallingwater" at Mill Run. This unique house was designed by Frank Lloyd Wright in 1936 and is now maintained by the Western Pennsylvania Conservancy. Left: Golden light splashes through Autumn foliage at Lake Jean, Ricketts Glen State Park. Pages 8 and 9 following: Fall colors enhance the pastoral beauty of farms in the Susquehanna River Valley near North Towanda. It drains a major segment of the state and flows majestically through rich farmlands.

A blanketed horse waits patiently on a cold November day for its Amish owner near Bartville. Left: Pennsylvania's forests have more deer than any other single state in the nation. This curious white tail doe comes to within a few feet of the photographer along the Loyalsock River Valley. Pages 12 and 13 following: Amish farmers toil long hours to harvest their winter crops at Christiana.

Passing storm reveals a brightly illuminated corn field near Lamar. Right: Betsy Ross House in Philadelphia. This well preserved home calls to mind the leading role played by the state of Pennsylvania in the drama of American history.

A young Amish gentleman
takes his courting buggy out
on a rainy Sunday near
Strasburg.

In the Pennsylvania Dutch region of Berks County, six miles west of the Schuylkill River and just off Interstate 78, surrounded by tall corn and tawny wheat, is an ancient German town called Shartlesville. On its one main street is an old inn with a weathered facade. The inn has a rickety front porch with peeling dark green paint, whitewashed plaster walls, dark green trim around the window frames and eaves, and a neon beer sign hanging in the tavern window on the left side of the porch.

On the right side of the porch is a dining room which serves "all-you-can-eat" country breakfasts for about $5. The size and astonishing beauty of these breakfasts is hard to believe.

A traveler is less apt to spend the $5 for a breakfast there than are the local laborers and farmhands, who really need the food for sustenance. They enter in their faded work clothes and muddy boots, greet the waitress as an old friend, and then the four of them sit down in creaking chairs to a long rectangular wooden table dark with age.

In the next ten or fifteen minutes, the waitress covers the entire table with huge steaming platters of scrambled eggs, pancakes, sausage, bacon, ham, scrapple, fried potatoes, coffeecake, and toast; bowls of applesauce and relish; jugs of coffee, orange juice, ice water, and milk, as well as syrup, butter, and jams. The men begin to eat a breakfast that could easily feed a crowd of 20. The platter of scrambled eggs alone must be a foot and a half long and eight or ten inches deep, the eggs bright yellow against the dark wood of the table and the white of the plate. The orange juice being poured from the tin jug beaded with moisture looks like the most refreshing orange juice ever served. The whole abundant scene is straight out of a 16th century Flemish painting.

The breakfast being served in Shartlesville is only one small isolated scene out of millions of different scenes taking place at the same hour across the vast expanse of this diversified state.

A few hours from now, 250 miles away in downtown Pittsburgh, a fashionably dressed luncheon crowd will be dining under exotic indoor trees at an unusual modern shopping mall created inside a 19th century bank, where one of the shops is a jewelry store built inside the bank's original vault. In the same city, steelworkers at U.S. Steel or aluminum workers at Alcoa will be eating sandwiches out of lunch pails. In downtown Lancaster, a varied crowd of Amish and Mennonite farmers and suburban housewives will be selecting vegetables and meats from the stalls at the Lancaster Farmers Market for their evening meals. Players on the Pittsburgh Pirates or Philadelphia Phillies baseball teams may be heading out to their respective modern parks for afternoon or evening games. Meanwhile, ships will be loading and unloading their cargoes, coming and going from such busy ports as Erie, on the Great Lakes, Pittsburgh at the fork of the Monongahela, Allegheny, and Ohio rivers, and Philadelphia on the Delaware and Schuylkill rivers, receiving iron ore from Minnesota or South America and shipping steel, coal, oil, and thousands of other goods and products to near and far parts of the world.

It is virtually impossible to condense the atmosphere of Pennsylvania into one convenient scene. To depict all of it would require a huge mural or an epic poem such as Walt Whitman's *Leaves of Grass*. The state is possibly the most intriguingly diversified of all the states. Its industry is phenomenal. The statistics one can muster to convince the sceptic of its wealth are overwhelming. Pittsburgh alone produces more manufactured goods in a year than 36 separate states. It offers everything from fine lace to atomic engines. Its ships carry more tonnage each year than all the ships passing through the Panama Canal.

But it is really Pennsylvania's people, from the farmhands eating breakfast in Shartlesville, to the Amish farmer plowing his fields with mules and smoking a cigar, to the persistent residents of Johnstown, stubbornly determined to rebuild their city after the third disastrous flood there in less than 90 years—Pennsylvania's men, women, and children of various national origins, the dwellings they inhabit and the regions they call home, which give this great state the distinctly *human* flavor that makes it so appealing and unique.

Yes, everywhere one looks in Pennsylvania, contrasts between city and country, industry and agriculture, new and old abound.

Of its 26 million acres stretching rectangularly from the Delaware River west to Lake Erie, and from the Mason-Dixon Line on its southern border north to New York State, over half of Pennsylvania (57 percent, to be exact) is still covered with woods. As urban, suburban, and industrial as Pennsylvania is, it also has the second largest rural population of any state in the nation.

Pennsylvania's wilderness is so robust that it shares with Texas the distinction of sheltering the most deer in the U.S. An average 120,000 white-tail deer, which is the state animal, are brought down by hunters each fall. It has been estimated that another 24,000 deer are killed annually on Pennsylvania's highways. The wild turkey hunting here is the best in North America. State game farms release each year over half a million pheasants, while hatcheries replenish the streams with two and a half million trout. On Hawk Mountain between Pottsville and Allentown as many as 3,000 eagles, ospreys, peregrine falcons, and turkey vultures have been sighted migrating south from Canada in one day.

Pennsylvania has entire counties of overwhelming beauty such as Lancaster, Chester, and Bucks, and industrial cities such as Scranton and Johnstown, which to the outsider appear bleak. The state has three unsurpassed river systems—the Delaware, Susquehanna, and Ohio—which at the same time have all caused terrible tragedies in the form of floods. Pennsylvania's famous anthracite and bituminous coal has heated millions of American homes, provided fuel for hundreds of electric power plants, been instrumental in the form of coke in the development of Pennsylvania's mightly steel industry, while its by-products have been used in everything from plastic to aspirin. The state's steel supports the Brooklyn Bridge, Holland and Lincoln Tunnels, and over a third of every steel structure and product in America. Yet the pay for Pennsylvania's steelworkers was once so low that their rage culminated in the Homestead Strike at the Carnegie Steel plant in Pittsburgh in 1892, one of the bitterest disputes in American labor history. At present, Pennsylvania's steel industry is in the grips of a serious financial crisis brought on by competition from low-cost imported steel (in the third quarter of 1977 Bethlehem Steel suffered a record $400 million loss). Not all of Pennsylvania's history has been roses. Like any state or country, like all humanity, it has had to accept its share of bad as well as good.

Pennsylvania (or *Pennsilvania* as it was originally spelled). The name is Latin for "Penn's Woods".

The state owes much of its past and present variety to one of American history's greatest men, the Quaker William Penn. Today, the "Quaker State" has approximately 12,000,000 residents (fourth largest in the United States). Many of them are descended from families which fled from tremendous religious persecution in Europe during the 17th and 18th centuries and settled in Pennsylvania as a result of Penn's broadmindedness.

The state was named, not for Penn himself, but for his father, Sir William Penn.

Sir William, a British admiral and war hero, had helped restore King Charles II to the throne in 1660 following the Puritan dictatorship of Oliver Cromwell. For his political loyalty, Penn was knighted by the king and promised a reward of £16,000. Sir William died in 1670, and the king, with the authority vested in him, could easily have overlooked the debt. Instead, he chose to repay the £16,000 by giving his friend's son a huge tract of land in the new World, thus making Penn the largest landowner in English history. But the land was surely worth more than £16,000. Why did the king give it away? Far from being totally generous, his decision was at least in part politically motivated.

King Charles II was a Catholic by inclination, and he was at odds throughout his reign with the religiously intolerant Anglican Cavalier Parliament. Numerous religious minority groups with which the king sympathized were being persecuted under Parliament's harsh Clarendon Code. For instance, between 1660 and 1680 some 11,000 Quakers were jailed. Many of the king's best friends, among them the stiff-necked William Penn (who in Quaker fashion refused to doff his hat in the king's presence), were religious nonconformists. It is generally agreed that the tolerant and pleasure-loving king (known to history as "The Merry Monarch") gave Penn the magnificent tract of land in America as a refuge for his friends and as a way of retaliating against the loathsome narrowness of his own Parliament.

Whatever his motives were, King Charles II made a brilliant choice in selecting Penn as the territory's landlord. Penn was 37 years old when he received the grant in 1681, and he was already a skilled leader, writer, diplomat, and businessman. He had been a religious rebel since his college days, when he was expelled from Oxford in his second year for his nonconformist views. He had then studied in France under a famous Protestant theologian and moved on to Ireland to manage his father's estates. It was there, in 1666-67, that Penn converted to Quakerism and became an outspoken advocate for the Society of Friends. In 1668 he was imprisoned for ten months in the Tower of London for writing a Quaker tract against the doctrine of the Trinity. In the next 14 years, before he ever sailed to America, he was arrested and jailed many times again. Between 1675 and 1681, aside from preaching the Quaker doctrine throughout England, Germany, and the Netherlands, he also wrote dozens of articles and books and managed to become one of the trustees of West Jersey and part owner of New Jersey.

Thus prepared for his greatest challenge, Penn sent envoys ahead of him to begin supervising the construction of Philadelphia (the first city ever built with its streets and avenues converging at right angles, a plan which Penn himself devised). Then in early October, 1682, he set sail for Pennsylvania on the "Welcome" and made ready to put his "holy experiment" into effect.

As Penn conceived of it, Pennsylvania would be a radical departure from strife-torn Europe, a peaceful land open to all religious groups, with a modern capital called "The City of Brotherly Love". It was an idealistic, even a mystical, conception. But Penn was a practical mystic, and, on the whole, considering the Utopian projects in America which have failed, his plan succeeded.

Thomas Jefferson called Penn "the greatest law-giver the world has produced". During his brief year and a half stay in Pennsylvania (he was to see it only once again, in 1699-1701, before his death in 1718), Penn created a radically liberal penal code, abolishing the death penalty for all crimes except murder and treason, which in its day was a great humanitarian advance. He dealt fairly with the Indians by buying rather than conquering their lands, thus insuring peace in the colony for the next 80 years. And, as he had promised, he opened the doors of Pennsylvania to a wide variety of oppressed religious groups.

Before Penn sailed up the Delaware River and landed at Upland (now Chester) on October 27, 1682, little progress had been made in the region by either the Swedes, Dutch or English for nearly 40 years. Now, with incredible speed, Pennsylvania blossomed into the democratic showpiece of the Western world.

Change happened so rapidly that by the time Penn returned in 1699, Philadelphia already ranked second in size to Boston in the Colonies. It was a beautiful town with slate-roofed brick houses separated by green yards. In designing it, Penn had been conscious of the terrible fire that had destroyed London in 1666, and also perhaps of the great London plague of 1665 which had snuffed out 75,000 lives. This is the reason Philadelphia was built of fire-resistant brick and slate and why the dwellings were separated by yards.

By the mid-1700s, Philadelphia had grown into the second largest English-speaking city, next to London, in the British Empire. The liberal atmosphere attracted many of the best minds in the Colonies and abundant talent from abroad. In this group was Robert Morris of Liverpool, later to become the "financier of the American Revolution", and the firebrand and pamphleteer Thomas Paine. Benjamin Franklin, who moved from Boston to Philadelphia in 1723, brought terrific energy to bear on improving his adopted city. He led the drive to have its streets paved, lighting system modernized, fire fighting and insurance companies organized, postal system improved, and he also established the first lending library in America and two of its greatest intellectual institutions, namely the American Philosophical Society and the University of Pennsylvania. He also raised the funds to build what has since become the oldest hospital in America.

One might say that Franklin took the rough clay that Penn had handed him and shaped it into polished form. But it was Penn who conceived the plan for the entire colony, and his influence on both the colony and the state of Pennsylvania was long lasting. The critical American historian Henry Adams judged the Pennsylvania of 1800 the "only true democratic community . . . the ideal American state, easy, tolerant, and contented".

It was Penn's religious openmindedness which led the Amish, Mennonites, Moravians, and Pietists to settle here, giving much of Pennsylvania a distinct Germanic character to this day. By 1776, one third of Pennsylvania's population came from German stock. While overzealous Puritans in Massachusetts were executing religious nonconformists in the Salem Witch Trials of 1692, Pennsylvania already embodied most of the democratic principles on which the nation would be founded.

"Proclaim Liberty throughout all the land unto all the Inhabitants Thereof." These are the words that Pennsylvanians chose from Leviticus to adorn the huge bell which was cast in the early 1750s to celebrate the 50th anniversary of Penn's great liberal constitution, the Charter of Privileges. Later rung in Philadelphia in July of 1776 to announce the Declaration of Independence, it has since become a symbol of American liberty as a whole.

From the Revolution onward, Pennsylvania acquired its familiar nickname as "The Keystone State".

The original 13 states formed a kind of arch along the Atlantic seaboard, and Pennsylvania was geographically the central state or keystone in the arch, binding the whole.

It was, first of all, the dividing line between the North and the South. In the 19th century, as tension mounted between the slave states and the free states, the Mason-Dixon Line on Pennsylvania's southern border came to symbolize the barrier between two irreconcilable ways of life. Pennsylvania was where the industrial North collided with the agrarian South. It was the focal point of abolitionist ferment, where leaders of the underground railroad worked incessantly to sneak runaway slaves across the Mason-Dixon Line into the free North. But controversy over the border line between Pennsylvania and Maryland began long before the conflict between North and South. . . . In 1684, William Penn became embroiled in a bitter legal argument with Charles Calvert, 3rd Lord Baltimore and proprietor of Maryland, over the boundary separating their lands. The two men carried on the dispute for years in London courts. The problem was not solved, however, until their descendants hired the British astronomers Charles Mason and Jeremiah Dixon to survey the land. The Mason-Dixon survey was conducted between 1763-67, and the final boundary line between Pennsylvania, Maryland, and Virginia (now West Virginia) was not completed until 1779.

Later, when Robert E. Lee took a wild gamble in the summer of 1863, crossed the Mason-Dixon Line and met the Union forces at Gettysburg, the confrontation was one of the bloodiest in modern history. Over 50,000 soldiers lost their lives.

Pennsylvania was also a "keystone" as the dividing line between civilized America and the Western frontier. It soon became a launching pad for the pioneers' grueling journey West. German gunsmiths in Lancaster County provided the pioneers with deadly-accurate Pennsylvania rifles, while Lancaster's wagonmakers stepped up production of their rugged Conestoga wagons. Pennsylvania's Daniel Boone blazed a trail through the

Cumberland Gap and led settlers down through southwestern Pennsylvania, western Virginia, and into Kentucky. When the Pennsylvania Canal finally crossed the almost impenetrable barrier of Allegheny Mountain and reached Pittsburgh in 1834, the city gained its reputation as "The Gateway To The West" almost overnight.

Economically, Pennsylvania has nearly always been America's "keystone" as the state with the best transportation systems (from the 1790s with the first toll road in America, the Lancaster Pike—to the 19th century with the best railroad in the world, the Pennsylvania Railroad, nicknamed "The Standard of the World"—to the 20th century with America's first superhighway, the Pennsylvania Turnpike). Due to the efficiency of these carrying systems, Pennsylvania has also had the most accessible mineral resources and the greatest industrial clout. It is only since World War II that Western states such as California and Texas have surpassed it in productivity.

But during America's crucial formative years, Pennsylvania was always *the* big state on which the nation's liberty hinged. Had Robert E. Lee defeated the Union forces at the battle of Gettysburg, and then pressed his advantage and overrun the state, the South would probably have won the Civil War. Pennsylvania produced 80 percent of the North's war resources. The state's iron, steel, coal, locomotives, and munitions earned it then, as well as later, the title, "The Arsenal of Democracy".

Pennsylvania was also America's "Arsenal" during the Revolutionary War, providing American troops with guns, cannons, uniforms, and food. More battles were fought within a 50-mile radius of Philadelphia than in all the New England states combined. Philadelphia was where the rebel Congress of Adams, Jefferson, and Franklin convened. It was the Colonial center of commerce, learning, and the arts—the "Athens of America"—the city that the British coveted the most. In defending it, George Washington was successful at first and then suffered a number of serious defeats. On Christmas Eve, 1776, he crossed the icy Delaware River from Bucks County and caught the British napping at the battles of Trenton and Princeton, both in New Jersey. But in the late summer and early fall of 1777, he lost two crucial battles at Brandywine and Germantown, lost Philadelphia to the British, and in the process almost lost his job as Commander in Chief of the American forces. He rallied following the severe winter encampment at Valley Forge, located only a dozen miles west of Philadelphia, and from then on his stature in the eyes of both his troops and his Congressional employers steadily rose.

The names of all these incidents and battles have since become so famous in American history, learned so early in life by most of us as reluctant students, that to many Americans they hardly seem real. Hardly real, that is, until one visits the actual sites and sees how much of Pennsylvania's history has been preserved.

For instance, at the Brandywine Battlefield in Chadds Ford, Chester County, there is an inventive stone farmhouse, not replica, where the Marquis de Lafayette made his headquarters during the battle and nursed his wounded leg. One can imagine Lafayette's aristocratic presence, his dismay or his tremendous sense of adventure at finding himself in such a crude new country so far away from the comforts of home. The farmhouse has stark white plaster walls, low ceilings and cramped rooms, a feeling of Quaker simplicity and purity, and an incredibly inefficient wood-lined chimney which on winter nights must have chilled its inhabitants to the bone. But it is the real thing, not a Hollywood stage set or a picture of the battle stamped on an imitation pewter plate.

In southern Bucks County on the Delaware River, the visitor may have a harder time imagining Washington crossing the ice-caked river with his shivering troops. The famous painting of the crossing gets in the way (a reproduction of it hangs in a modern building there), and the many tourists wandering through the park tend to detract from the atmosphere. But the Delaware River is still there; one can see exactly how wide it is and get a fairly good idea of how long it must have taken Washington to cross it. Surprisingly, the river is not that wide. The myth of the crossing has swelled its width in the imagination to oceanic proportions, as if Washington were still crossing it today and had never reached the other side! Seeing it brings one blessedly back to earth, makes Washington more of a real man and less of a demigod, and gives one, for a fleeting instant, a sudden spark of connection between the present and the past.

Virtually the same observations can be made about hundreds of historically interesting places throughout the state. Old and familiar though Pennsylvania's history is, it springs to life when one is there. From Independence Hall in Philadelphia, immaculately preserved, with the same floors, walls, and bricks that housed a Congress which excited lovers of democracy around the world, all the way across the state to the amazing Horseshoe Curve at Altoona, to Drake's oil well at Titusville, even to the existing steel mills at Pittsburgh, one is constantly reminded of America's past.

Of all the regions in Pennsylvania where history is still very much alive, perhaps the most intriguing is Lancaster County. It is here the long, long ago, spills over into the present every second of every day.

Lancaster County is one of the richest farming areas in the world—a miracle of growth. Located 70 miles due west of Philadelphia and 50 miles east of the state capital at Harrisburg, it is also an ideal place for light and heavy industry. The county's fertile limestone soil has been augmented over the years by alluvium from the Susquehanna River on its western border. Agriculturally, it is just about the closest thing to heaven on earth. An awesome sense of German meticulousness appears in its geometrically perfect rows of wheat, tobacco, and corn; its beautiful fat cows; its freshly painted barns, their tin silos gleaming in the sun; plus the astonishing freshness, colorfulness, and cleanliness of the produce at the Lancaster Farmer's Market located just off the central square downtown .

"Whenever I visit Lancaster," said a friend employed in Harrisburg, "I'm always overcome by a terrible sense of guilt at my own sloth. The work ethic there is just tremendous."

Here, as almost everybody knows, people from the Old Order of the Amish sect still dress, worship, farm, and travel as their ancestors did 250 years ago. There are sects such as the Dunkers and River Brethren which baptize their children outdoors by immersion, even if the ice must be cracked. The so-called "Black Bumper Mennonites" drive black automobiles with all the chrome painted black. Some Amish even refuse to buy insurance or lightning rods, feeling both would be a thwarting of God's will. Young Amish men begin to grow beards on their wedding day, but throughout their lives they shave their upper lips. Instead of wearing buttons on their vests and jackets, they use hook and eyes. Both customs originate from the fact that the Amish, like the Quakers, have always been staunch pacifists. In the Germany of the late 1600s and 1700s, military men sported bristling mustaches and gaudy buttons on their uniforms. In reaction, Amish men shaved their upper lips and swore off using buttons.

The Old Order Amish still live without electricity, telephones, tractors or automobiles. Yet some Amish farmers are not above using engine-powered planting and harvesting equipment, which they pull along incongruously with horses or mules. Their gleaming black-lacquered horsedrawn buggies with freshly painted gray canvas tops are a familiar sight in old German townships such as Bird-In-Hand, Intercourse, New Holland, and Paradise. Amish couples and families trot along the roads and highways seemingly oblivious to the line of cars and tour buses following behind them. While cars pull up to gas stations for refueling, Amish horses stand munching oats from feed bags as their owners shop in stores. One is apt to find more working blacksmith shops in Lancaster County than in almost any county in the U.S. In downtown Lancaster, Amish and Mennonite farmers with their flowing beards, black broad-brimmed hats, and austere black clothes stroll the busy sidewalks side by side with businessmen in three-piece suits.

Yet, in spite of their refusal to adopt modern ways and modern tools, the Amish and Mennonites are among America's cleverest and most productive farmers. Not all the farmers in Lancaster adhere to the old ways, and many of the Mennonites belong to liberal sects as modern as most conventional Protestant churches. In any case, the county's farmers are so hard-working that Lancaster leads all counties in the nation in farm production on non-irrigated land. Every inch of space here seems to be put to use. The county's 6,000 farms, valued at over $2 billion, yield $350 million a year in crops, dairy products, livestock, and poultry. Lancaster County is second in the nation in dairy production and fifth in the cultivation of tobacco. Amish men smoke stogies, a derivative from the rough teamsters who used to smoke coarse cigars while driving Conestoga wagons, but otherwise their vices are few. There are approximately 230,000 steers on county livestock farms, 135,000 hogs, and 23,000,000 chickens! Lancaster County also boasts the largest terminal livestock market in the East, and its magnificent auction market in New Holland is one of the largest in the world.

But for all its agricultural wealth, the county produces industrial goods valued at $2.5 billion yearly, eight times the value of its agriculture. These range from floor products at the Armstrong cork plant, to electric shavers at Schick, to mobile homes, to agricultural machinery in New Holland. The county has a huge modern shopping mall (Park City) and a suburban business strip (the Columbia Pike) crammed with gas stations and quick food stands. Land in the county is so sought after by business and residential real estate developers, that young Amish families are having to move elsewhere to farm. As if its great agricultural and industrial productivity weren't enough, Lancaster County is also one of the ten leading tourist attractions in America. Visitors love the fact that the Amish refused to merge along with everybody else in the great American melting pot. The wonderful surprise of Lancaster, in spite of its growing commercialism, is that it is a truly different world, maintaining a *living continuation of the past.*

Lancaster's appealing regional uniqueness is a quality which repeats itself with amazing frequency throughout the state. Unlike New England, where Colonial architecture varies only slightly from town to town, the Pennsylvania "image" is much harder to pin down.

Is the classic Pennsylvania structure a red Pennsylvania Dutch barn decorated with a hex sign, or is it a refined 18th century fieldstone manor house in Chester or Bucks County? Is it a covered bridge, of which Pennsylvania has more than any other state, or is it the old red brick of Philadelphia's Elfreth's Alley and Independence Hall? Is it the German architecture of a wonderful village such as Lititz in Lancaster County, where the whole town is enveloped with the smell of chocolate from the candy factory when the wind is right, or Shartlesville with its ancient inn and abundant food?

Look through almost any bookstore in the state. There are virtually no popular books in print which have as their subject Pennsylvania as a whole. Pennsylvania writers seem to be more interested in describing their own regions. In Bucks County one finds books on the county's history, its stone architecture, the Bucks County Playhouse, or the Delaware Canal. Bucks was one of the three original counties layed out by William Penn; (Philadelphia and Chester are the other two). Its venerable bluestocking families, its artists, writers, craftsmen, and musicians, its prosperous Philadelphia lawyers and businessmen, all these people, many of them highly sophisticated and cultured, others pretending to be so, are vastly different from the majority of residents in Lancaster County, even though the counties are only 70 miles apart.

There are even striking differences from county to county between the so-called "Pennsylvania Dutch". The term is really a mispronunciation of the word for German, *Deutsch.* The various religious sects of Lancaster County have traditionally been lumped together as the "Plain People" or "Plain Dutch", due to their plain style of dress. In Reading and surrounding Berks County, the majority of German descendents dress in modern or "fancy" clothes and are referred to as the "Gay People" or "Gay Dutch". Many of them think of themselves as earthier, happier, bawdier, and less restrained than their neighbors in Lancaster. Thus, a Reading-ite may laugh up his sleeve at the severe lifestyle of an Amishman from Lancaster. The Amishman may in turn shake his head at what he feels to be the coarseness and worldliness of the man from Reading. And a native of Bucks County may find the ways of both, quite quaint perhaps, but also a bit provincial. All three people will dress differently, talk and worship differently, and eat different foods.

Such regional differences make visiting Pennsylvania a fascinating experience. Everywhere one goes, one is very likely to stumble on something unexpected and new.

The 300-mile drive from Philadelphia to Pittsburgh might just as well be 3,000 miles for all the cultural similarities between the two. The rivalry between Lancaster and Reading pales before the rivalry between old, established, Eastern Philadelphia and bold, industrial, Western Pittsburgh. Here, in one state, sliced diagonally in half by the Allegheny Mountains, begins the rivalry which characterizes America as a whole. Pennsylvania is East *and* West, and partly South, too.

There is a distinct Southernness to much of Pennsylvania's vegetation. Most of the trees and plants in bordering Maryland and Virginia also appear in the southern half of Pennsylvania. The towering tulip poplars are the first trees which come to mind. Wild, choking honeysuckle climbing fences, wires and telephone poles. In Bucks County, driving on Route 32 from New Hope to Point Pleasant along the Delaware Canal, are woods as damp, green, shadowy, and teeming with plant life as anywhere in the Deep South. Sycamore, locust, black walnut, sassafras, catalpa, dogwood, mountain laurel, mimosa, swarming with wild grape vines and buzzing with insect sounds. If you stake a tent in any one of Buck's many campgrounds, even on a crystal clear night, expect to wake up in the morning soaked and totally uncomfortable from the humidity.

But there is nothing at all Southern about Bucks' fieldstone houses and barns. They crop up around every bend in the road —mansions, farmhouses, taverns—built with amazing skill out of red sandstone, buff shale or gray gneiss, with neat mortar "pointing" between the stones, creating the impression of an insoluble puzzle or intricate system of veins. The reason that the Quaker settlers here built with stone, even though wood was plentiful and their countrymen in New England were building with wood, is that they came from regions in the British Isles such as Wiltshire and the Cotswolds where stone architecture was predominant. Looking at such buildings here and in Chester County, one suddenly thinks that Pennsylvania's greatest artists were its stonemasons, as skilled in their own way as the cathedral builders of medieval Europe. Then, just as suddenly, one recalls the great wooden tobacco barns of Lancaster County, with their tall drying panels open on a summer afternoon and the green tobacco leaves hanging inside. It would be too narrow to classify either as "the greatest" art. Both are uniquely beautiful in their own ways.

Perhaps more than the residents of any county in Pennsylvania, the people of Bucks seem to be the most obsessed with preserving their past. They may drive to Philadelphia and work in modern office buildings by day, but when they get home, they want their comfort old. Preservation and restoration require money, of course, and Bucks has always been blessed with that ingredient. New Hope on the Delaware Canal is popular with summer tourists, theatre-goers, and artists, but some of its charm has been tarnished by commercialism and crowds. The real jewel of the county is Doylestown, the county seat.

Arriving in Doylestown is like stepping into a time machine and being suddenly whirled 200 years into the past. Unlike Virginia's recreated Williamsburg, where one pays admission to walk around, Doylestown is free and still a working town. Lawyers, dentists, and doctors have their shingles out, and business proceeds as usual at the county courthouse. But the courthouse, built in 1960, is a minor miracle of modern architecture, its stainless steel, glass, and red brick somehow blend perfectly with the Colonial atmosphere of the town. There doesn't seem to be a speck of dust on any of Doylestown's narrow streets. The whole town gleams. Street after street is lined with low, slate-roofed row houses built of clean, sandblasted red and orange brick, with freshly painted doors and window frames, with doorknobs, door knockers, and outside lanterns gleaming with polished brass. An incredible amount of care and money has gone into preserving the original character of the town.

Doylestown also has an astonishing museum containing perhaps more early American artifacts than any museum of its kind. It is a towering neo-Florentine affair built in 1913 out of reinforced concrete. Called the Mercer Museum, it was conceived and designed by Dr. Henry Chapman Mercer, a noted anthropologist who inherited a fortune and spent it on buying up the past. Housed beneath the museum's imposing roof is a treasure trove of 17th, 18th, and 19th century pre-industrial Americana. Here the visitor finds everything from cigar store Indians and ancient fireman's hats, dating back to Benjamin Franklin's day, plus funeral caskets and a full size working gallows. Henry Ford called it "the only museum in America which I am sufficiently interested in enough to visit".

Roving the surrounding countryside, Dr. Mercer would collect old axes by the dozens, old wood stoves, cast iron fireplates, swords, pistols, and rifles by the hundreds. One of everything was not enough to satisfy his soul. Eclectic to a fault, he seized on whale boats, Conestoga wagons, sleighs, buggies, and carriages of all kinds. The museum contains hundreds of thousands of these old conveyances, knicknacks, and tools. It is, possibly, the best stocked attic in the world. As in any great museum, the onlooker gradually grows weary and ashamed by the plenitude of things. Two hours is not nearly enough time to absorb what the museum contains and means. The visitor climbs the four or five floors of the medieval interior with growing wonder and dismay, passing 18th century lock shops, candle shops, print shops, blacksmith shops, hinge shops, shoe shops, engraving shops with every one of them filled to bursting with the appropriate tools. On the top floor, as if the visitor had climbed through all the stages of life and were now prepared to enter heaven or descend to hell, is Dr. Mercer's collection of straw caskets and funeral equipment, as well as his wooden gallows with its chilling trap door.

Mercer's staggering museum is a fitting symbol of Pennsylvania's seemingly endless variety. It is also appropriate that it was erected in Doylestown, at the very center of Bucks County, where people care so much about preserving the past.

Yet, again, exactly as in Lancaster County, Bucks is not exclusively countrified, manorial, and divorced from modern life. Bordering on Philadelphia to the south and the Bethlehem-Allentown area to the north, Bucks also has the huge U.S. Steel plant at Fairless Hills on the Delaware River, as well as one of the best known symbols of modern suburban America, a sprawling Levittown development. Then again, almost within walking distance of U.S. Steel, is tranquil Pennsbury Manor, a recreation of William Penn's beautiful estate in the New World. Five minutes away, a stream of traffic roars to and from Philadelphia on Route 13. Yet here at Pennsbury are spacious lawns, great shade trees, fine old 17th century brick buildings, and, best of all, whole flocks of turkeys, ducks, and wildly squawking guinea hens roaming the lawns.

To embark on the Pennsylvania Turnpike from cultivated Bucks County towards the Northern and Western regions of the state, is like passing from 18th century agrarian America into a newer, bold world.

Cities such as Scranton, Wilkes-Barre, Johnstown, and Pittsburgh really started booming during the Industrial Revolution. Things happened in these regions before the 1830s, but never so swiftly as they did once the canals and the iron horse arrived.

Western Pennsylvania began to flex its muscles as early as the Whiskey Rebellion of 1794, when the fiercely independent Scotch-Irish frontiersmen living west of the Allegheny Mountains refused to pay their taxes to the young and struggling federal government in Philadelphia. Western resentment against the Eastern quarter of the state grew so strong that the state capital was moved west to Lancaster in 1799 and then farther west to Harrisburg in 1812.

While not exactly "Western" in location, Harrisburg was just far enough west at the turn of the 19th century to be beyond the main line of transportation to and from the state's commercial hub at Philadelphia. First settled in 1710, it did not rise to full prosperity until the arrival of the Pennsylvania Canal in 1827 and the railroad in 1836. The building of the state-owned Pennsylvania Canal from Philadelphia to Pittsburgh in the 1820s and 1830s, and the subsequent linking of both cities by the Pennsylvania Railroad in the middle 1850s, transformed the face of Pennsylvania and unlocked roughly 90 percent of its great untapped natural resources.

Pennsylvania's steel, coal, oil, and wood were sorely needed by the rapidly expanding industrial nation. Fabulous fortunes would soon be made by such Pittsburgh titans of industry and high finance as Andrew Carnegie, Andrew Mellon, Henry Clay Frick, and Charles M. Schwab. By the Civil War, Pennsylvania had become the first boom state in the U.S. By the late 1860s, it already had America's first ghost town, Pithole, which in 1865 provided over half the world's supply of oil, and a year later didn't have a drop of oil left.

The boom attracted draftdodgers and rogues as awful as John Wilkes Booth, actor and Confederate sympathizer, who came to the oil fields of Venango County to strike it rich and shortly afterward assasinated President Abraham Lincoln at Ford's Thea-

tre on April 14, 1865. Perhaps one of the saddest moments in our nation's early history.

But it also attracted a whole new wave of European immigrants. Someone has estimated that Pittsburgh's present population of 2,500,000 people derives from as many as 77 different ethnic groups! This same rich ethnic mixture even appears in an industrial city as old as Bethlehem, first settled by German Moravians in the early 1700s, but diversified over the last century by Slovaks, Hungarians, Croatians, Alsatians, Greeks, Carpatho-Russians, Poles, and, the newest arrivals, Puerto Ricans.

Many of these people may have come to Pennsylvania hoping for overnight wealth, but what they found was hard labor toiling in steel mills, coal mines, saw mills, cement plants and glass factories, and especially on the railroad. It took thousands of men to build the Pennsylvania Canal system, and many thousands more to cut the Pennsylvania Railroad through the Allegheny Mountains in the days before the steam shovel. The problem of getting the canal and then the railroad over or through the 36-mile stretch of mountains from Altoona to Johnstown was tremendous.

Since roughly three-fourths of Pennsylvania is either hilly or mountainous, and since mountains have played such a crucial role in the development of the state, the Allegheny Mountains assume a position of prime importance.

Rich in coal, but a severe obstacle to transportation, the Alleghenies are part of the long, old, rugged Appalachian Mountains which first crop up in Maine and extend all the way to Alabama. They are famous for their hardwood forests, wildlife, and scenic beauty, but never attempt to tell that to an engineer faced with the problem of tunneling a road through them. Technically, the Alleghenies begin in the northeastern corner of the state with the Poconos, but they reach their full height about 100 miles west of Harrisburg in a plateau so sheer that it has been known for centuries as Allegheny Mountain. The mountain cuts straight down through central Pennsylvania from the New York border to the Maryland line. In Somerset County near Maryland it reaches its highest elevation at 3213 foot Mt. Davis, the highest point in the state. Transportation through the Alleghenies was no problem in Eastern and East-central Pennsylvania, because the Delaware and Susquehanna rivers cut spectacular water gaps through them, which made natural roads for early settlers and pioneers. But in West-central Pennsylvania, at Allegheny Mountain itself, there are no shortcuts. There is no getting *around* the mountain. It is fierce. Were it not for this steep wall which stands smack in the middle of the most direct route from Philadelphia to Pittsburgh, the western half of Pennsylvania might have been settled and developed much sooner that it was.

The first great feat of engineering accomplished in the Alleghenies was the building of the Allegheny Portage Railroad, completed between 1833-35. This was an incredibly complicated and expensive system devised to haul canal boats from the Pennsylvania Canal up over Allegheny Mountain starting near Altoona at Hollidaysburg and down the other side to Johnstown. A series of five inclined plains, or steps, was built on each side of the mountain. At the top of each step was a stationary steam engine which pulled the canal boats up by rail. On the level stretches between each inclined plain, the boats were pulled by horses and locomotives. A new kind of canal boat, built in several sections, had to be invented in order for the system to work efficiently. Such a boat would dock at Hollidaysburg in the morning, be dismantled into two, three or four pieces, and then be loaded onto separate flatbed cars. By noon the long grind up the steep face of Allegheny Mountain would begin. At the 2200-foot summit the crew on board the boat would rest overnight, resembling Noah stranded high and dry atop Mount Ararat, and in the morning they would begin their step by step descent to Johnstown, where the Western end of the canal waited to float them to Pittsburgh and parts West.

Charles Dickens rode the Portage Railroad in 1842, commenting that, "Occasionally the rails are laid upon the extreme verge of a giddy precipice and looking from the carriage window, the traveler gazes sheer down without a stone or scrap of fence between into the mountain depths below. The journey is very carefully made however . . . (and) not to be dreaded for its dangers." That was after the engineering genius John A. Roebling, who later designed the Brooklyn Bridge, suggested that wire cables, rather than hemp rope, be used to haul the carriages up or lower them down. But for the first seven years of operation, the mile-long hemp ropes were always wearing out and breaking. Accidents were numerous, and the railroad was never, as Dickens assumed, perfectly safe.

During its 20 years of cumbersome operation, the Allegheny Portage Railroad required 12 stationary steam engines, 12 different teams of horses, nine locomotives, and 54 workmen, all for the sole purpose of carrying canal boats just 36 miles. The state never made a profit on it, but it did serve its purpose of speeding up the transportation of goods and people between Eastern and Western Pennsylvania.

Today, all that remains of the Allegheny Portage Railroad is the imposing Samuel Lemon House at the summit of Allegheny Mountain and a few stone bridges and stone railroad ties. Samuel Lemon made a fortune selling coal and supplies to the railroad and providing services for passengers and workmen, and so his large fieldstone house survives. But the rest is as desolate as the ruins of Carthage or Troy. Like Pitthole, which once boasted 50 hotels and a population of 15,000 people, there is absolutely nothing left but grass and trees.

The usefulness of the Allegheny Portage Railroad was displaced in 1854 by the completion of the East-West line of the Pennsylvania Railroad. That was the year in which the Horseshoe Curve at Altoona was finished, and the railroad could now cross Allegheny Mountain without stopping. In its day, the Horseshoe Curve was widely regarded as one of the Seven Wonders of the industrial world.

A few miles west of Altoona, a shop town which ably served

as the repair center for the Pennsylvania Railroad's locomotives and cars, are two steeply-plunging mountains which could not be tunneled through nor spanned by a bridge. The only solution was to carve a fantastic curve along the mountain sides, with a huge dirt embankment between the mountains at the head of the curve to connect the two. It took a work force of thousands to build the curve with nothing more than picks and shovels. The curve is actually more constricted-looking than the name "horseshoe" implies. From the air, it looks like a long hairpin or a narrow capital U. It is an amazing phenomenon, located in the middle of nowhere, in incredibly rugged country, reached by car on a lonely, bumpy road. One wonders what to do once one arrives, except buy a candy bar and a postcard at the little gift shop and climb the towering embankment to gape at the curve. For some reason, the same atmosphere that prevails at the ruins of the Portage Railroad also prevails here. The Horseshoe Curve is still used, but the great days when the Pennsylvania Railroad was "The Standard of the World" have passed away. Since the demise of the Penn-Central, Conrail operates the once mighty system.

Horseshoe Curve, as well as long Gallitzin Tunnel which plunges through the mountain just beyond the western end of the curve, was such a crucial link in the railroad's East-West line that it was closed to civilians for security reasons during World War II. In June of 1942, a team of eight Nazi saboteurs landed in Florida by submarine. Among their objectives was the destruction of both Gallitzin Tunnel and Horseshoe Curve. Fortunately, the saboteurs were caught before they did any damage.

The building of the Portage Railroad and especially the completion of Horseshoe Curve turned Western Pennsylvania into a thriving region. Now Pittsburgh and Johnstown could produce goods which could be transported easily and cheaply to anywhere in the East or, for that matter, the West or the world.

Both cities were located almost right on top of huge bituminous coal beds. Driving through the Johnstown region today, one can see roadcuts streaked with veins of coal. Across the state, in anthracite-rich Scranton, the very earth is black with coal: the hills are not really hills but mounds of coal detritus; streets end abruptly in abandoned coal fields; strip mines sneak up almost to City Hall. The soft bituminous coal was ideal for the production of coke, which in turn could generate the tremendous degree of heat needed to operate the Bessemer steel furnaces which had just been introduced. The region also contained iron ore, although not of a very high grade.

Luckily, both cities were within striking distance of Lake Erie. Ships began to carry high-grade iron ore across the Great Lakes from Minnesota, where fabulous ore deposits had recently been unearthed. Trains then carried the ore from the port of Erie down to Pittsburgh and Johnstown. Pittsburgh was better situated, however, since it was closer to Lake Erie and located on three rivers, one of which stretched into the heart of the West. Within 40 years, from 1835 to 1875, Pittsburgh became both "The Gateway to the West" and "The Workshop of the World."

As a place to live, however, Pittsburgh was somewhat oppressive. This condition was dictated by the emissions from her industrial stacks. There was nothing old enough in Pittsburgh to match the cozy Colonial quality of Philadelphia or its surrounding villages and towns. The city was new and raw. Pittsburgh gained a reputation as a town of muscular men, where steel workers and coal miners ate raw steaks, burnt outside and cold red inside. As time wore on the city grew old, but still remained raw, with the darkness of its buildings turning from brown to black. Everything had been seemingly erected quickly, with no thought for the future and little regard for the past. The city's street and highway system, complicated by the presence of three rivers, was a major concern. Upon seeing Pittsburgh in 1935, architect Frank Lloyd Wright declared, "It would be cheaper to abandon it and build onother one."

But in the late 1940s, the city began to undergo a renaissance. Steps were taken to reduce the amount of rust-colored smoke belching from the chimneys of such companies as U.S. Steel and Jones & Laughlin Steel. Large sections of the downtown area were demolished and rebuilt. While people were still laughing at the very mention of the word "Pittsburgh", the city had changed dramatically.

The Pittsburgh of today leads all cities in the nation in air pollution control. Its streets, buildings, and houses are illuminated and have been for some time by the first commercial nuclear power plant in America. The "Golden Triangle" where the Allegheny and Monongahela rivers converge to form the Ohio, is now a modern shopping and financial district with soaring glass skyscrapers and a large park. Three Rivers Stadium where the Pittsburgh Pirates and the Pittsburgh Steelers play their games is one of the finest stadiums in the country. Pittsburgh has also become, not just "The Workshop of the World," but one of America's great money centers. It ranks third in the U.S. as a headquarters for major corporations. These include such giants as U.S. Steel, Gulf Oil, Westinghouse Electric, Alcoa Aluminum, National steel, and Jones and Laughlin Steel—100 major corporations in all. It is the nation's busiest inland port. It is also the world's largest manufacturer of steel, aluminum, plate and window glass, steel rolls, rolling mill machinery, and air brakes, as well as a leader in the production of cement and the processing of canned foods. Heinz pickles and the "57 Varieties" originate here.

Pittsburgh's most famous financiers, Andrew Carnegie and Andrew Mellon returned millions of their dollars back to the city in the form of universities, museums, libraries, and parks. The Carnegie Museum, with its wealth of classical and modern paintings, is one of the largest in the world. The Carnegie Library is well known as a center of scholarly research. Carnegie-Mellon University has great theatre and art departments and important medical and scientific research laboratories. The University of Pittsburgh and Duquesne University are also located here.

While visitors to modern Pittsburgh may be startled by its clean buildings and clear air, they might hesitate to agree with the constant flow of superlatives which issues from the typewriters at the chamber of commerce. Pittsburgh is a great city, and it is eager to attract new business and become greater still. But it is first and foremost America's mightiest industrial center, and not to be compared with Boston or San Francisco for culture or historical mellowness.

Johnstown, on the other hand, has suffered while Pittsburgh has thrived.

The worst flood in American history occurred there on that memorable day, May 31, 1889.

An 80-foot earth dam holding back an artificial lake four miles long by a mile wide, containing roughly 18 million tons of water, burst after 11 days of heavy rain. It unleashed a wall of water 30 to 40 feet high, traveling at a speed of 60 miles an hour, on hamlets surrounding Johnstown and finally on the city itself. The dam broke at three o'clock in the afternoon, and the flood caught almost everybody by complete surprise. The tidal wave of yellow-brown water picked up locomotives and passenger cars, houses, people, animals, trees, and logs, and launched the whole terrific pile of debris straight down the narrow South Fork and Conemaugh valleys onto Johnstown. The wreckage did not stop until it had destroyed most of the city, with a recorded population of approximately 28,000, and smashed into a stone arch bridge owned by the Pennsylvania Railroad. The bridge halted its flow, but then fire broke out. The logs and houses jammed against the bridge turned into an inferno which consumed hundreds of people struggling to keep afloat. The city's firefighting equipment had been destroyed, and survivors stood by helplessly listening to the screams. The final death toll was almost too painful to believe. Over 3,000 people lost their lives.

The worst of it was that the flood should never had occurred. Conemaugh Lake had been built in the late 1840s as a reservoir for the Western end of the Pennsylvania Canal. When the canal went out of business, the Pennsylvania Railroad picked it up.

Then in 1879 a group of Pittsburgh men purchased it for the South Fork Hunting and Fishing Club. The dam was badly in need of repair. A large iron grate had been installed at the top of the spillway to keep fish in. The grate was clogged, and as a result the dam lacked a crucial safety valve. Engineers had inspected it in the early 1880s and declared it unsafe and in need of alteration. So in a sense the flood was man made.

Johnstown was hit again by the "Saint Patrick's Day Flood" of 1936, but nobody was killed. Then on July 20, 1977, in the middle of the night, flash-flooding from the sides of the steep hills which surround and overshadow the town, located in what could be defined as a perilous gulch, suddenly swept houses and whole communities away. Over 100 people drowned. The irony is that, following the flood of 1936, the Army Corps of Engineers did extensive flood-prevention work in Johnstown. The city had earned a reputation as being almost flood proof. Nobody expected the rain to fall as hard as it did in July. A month later, when this writer visited Johnstown on August 18, it was still a disaster area. Most of the businesses in the downtown area were closed, their inventory ruined by water which had climbed five to six feet up the sides of buildings. Electrical power had only just been turned back on. The daily Johnstown-Tribune Democrat had just resumed publication after a month of silence. The Bethlehem Steel plant had been severely damaged, forcing nearly 4,000 people to be laid off. Due to the flood and the corporation's terrible financial year generally, Bethlehem officials decided not to go ahead with installation of a modern blast furnace, which would have meant more jobs for the town. Bulldozers were still working in the streets, their headlights on as night began to fall, scraping up mud and debris.

Halfway across the state, in the Great Valley, Lancaster County was on the verge of an abundant harvest. Only 20 miles away from Johnstown, in affluent Ligonier, with its white gazebo in the center square, with the lights in its expensive shops just beginning to come on, all was apparently well. But in Johnstown, where the sun seems to set an hour earlier than it should, located as it is in that shadowy gulch, with its ominous inclined plain on one side of the hills to carry people up to higher ground, the sense of desolation was overwhelming. An outsider, like Frank Lloyd Wright, might say, "It would be cheaper to abandon it, move it somewhere safer, and build another one." But outsiders are somewhat callous when it comes to understanding how deeply people feel about their roots. The residents of Johnstown had no intention of moving out. To them, for better or worse, there was no question that Johnstown was home.

Johnstown is not the only city in Pennsylvania which had suffered from severe floods. In fact, located as most of them are on rivers, nearly all the cities in the state have been hit. The worst flooding in recent years was caused by Hurricane Agnes in 1972. In that disaster, the Penn-Central Railroad alone suffered $20 million worth of damage and lost 48 bridges and buildings. Wilkes-Barre on the East Branch of the Susquehanna River was virtually destroyed.

Floods have always been a fact of life in Pennsylvania. Records dating back to 1786 describe the great "Pumpkin Floods" of that fall, when pumpkins came booming down the Susquehanna "like great orange cannon-balls and had much the same effect on horses and men who stood in the way . . . For two whole days the river looked as if a person could walk over it on pumpkins." In 1865, Pittsburgh experienced its great "Barrel Flood" when thousands of oil barrels from Vanango County's oil fields were swept down the Ohio River. But Pittsburgh's worst flood was the "Saint Patrick's Day Flood" of 1936. Eighty people died, 500 were injured, and approximately 135,000 were left homeless. Total property damage was estimatd at a quarter of a billion dollars.

But in spite of these disasters, Pennsylvanians have nearly always managed to repair the damage and come back strong. The flood which destroyed Wilkes-Barre, for instance, led to a massive urban renewal project which definitely improved the town. It takes more than devastating floods to uproot people from their homes.

Yes, there is so much more to tell about "The Keystone State" that a writer could spend a lifetime, fill a dozen books, and still not do it justice. Since each region, and even each county (the state has 63) is so distinctive, one could easily write a book about each place. And then another book about each city. And then additional books about particular aspects of each region, county and city.

While the task of "telling all" seems insurmountable, one feels compelled to say more. The reader should bear in mind, however, that the following annecdotes and facts are just a handful out of thousands one could relate . . .

It seems fitting, for instance, that the state which produced Andrew Carnegie, Andrew Mellon, and Joseph N. Pew, all of them heads of enormous vertical trusts, should also have produced the inventor of *Monopoly*, the world's most popular proprietary board game. Charles B. Darrow of Germantown, a witty man with a great imagination and time on his hands, invented the game while he was out of work during the Depression. Before the stock market crash of 1929, Darrow and his wife often vacationed in Atlantic City, New Jersey. Darrow named such coveted properties as Boardwalk, Park Place, and Marvin Gardens after streets and areas in the couple's favorite resort town. The railroads—the Pennsylvania, Baltimore & Ohio, Reading, and Short Line—seemed obvious since all traversed his own state. Darrow began by whittling the houses and hotels and making the boards and "Chance" and "Community Chest Cards" in his own home and giving them to friends. Then he started selling the game to Philadelphia department stores. He couldn't keep up with the popular demand so he sold the game to a major manufacturer in 1935.

Another interesting story, and far more crucial to the development of modern Pennsylvania, is how the Pennsylvania Turnpike got its start. The story, retreats all the way back to the 1800s —before anyone was even driving automobiles.

William H. Vanderbilt, son of the famous Commodore and head of the powerful New York Central Railroad, decided to build a railroad from Pittsburgh to Philadelphia to compete with the Pennsylvania Railroad. The man who gave him the idea was Franklin B. Gowen, president of the Reading Railroad, who conceived the scheme but didn't have the money to finance it. Andrew Carnegie and other Pittsburgh steel manufacturers got wind of the project and promptly bought several million dollars worth of stock. They had been complaining for years about the high rates that the Pennsylvania Railroad was charging to haul their steel east. With a $15 million dollar syndicate formed, $5 million of which was Vanderbilt's, the South Penn Railroad began to let out construction contracts in September, 1883. By September 1885, the South Penn was 60 percent completed, with six and a half miles of tunnels dug through the Allegheny Mountains, and 27 workers lost in blasting accidents and cave-ins. Vanderbilt, Carnegie, Gowen, and the other shareholders had by now spent $10 million on the project.

At this point, New York's financial wizard J. P. Morgan, who later bought out Carnegie's steel business for half a billion dollars and formed U.S. Steel, stepped in and advised Vanderbilt that his invasion of the Pennsylvania Railroad's territory was a destructive type of competition that would do neither railroad any good. Vanderbilt heard Morgan out and came to the conclusion that Morgan was correct. He then ordered Chauncey Depew, president of the New York Central, to try to work out a deal with George B. Roberts, president of the Pennsylvania Railroad. J. P. Morgan acted as the go-between. Morgan invited Roberts and Depew for a cruise up the Hudson River on his yacht, the "Corsair". In the course of the afternoon, Depew and Morgan managed to convince Roberts to accept the unfinished South Penn project in exchange for the West Shore Line in New York, a bankrupt line owned by the Pennsylvania Railroad and competing with the New York Central. The upshot of the story is that the Pennsylvania Railroad acquired the South Penn with no injury to its own freight business and no reductions in its rates. But Andrew Carnegie and other minority shareholders were so enraged that Vanderbilt and Morgan had not consulted them about the deal, that they brought a permanent injunction against the merger. Years later, when Carnegie sold Carnegie Steel to Morgan, he exacted his revenge by selling it for considerably more than it was worth. The injunction brought all work on the line to a halt. Carnegie and Gowen could have completed it themselves, but decided against it. In March, 1890, the property was auctioned off, and the defunct railroad became known as "Vanderbilt's Folly."

It was 45 years later, in the midst of the Depression, with thousands of Pennsylvanians out of work, that the idea of using the abandoned South Penn line as the basis for a modern superhighway across the state was suggested to Warren Van Dyke, Pennsylvania's Secretary of Highways, and Edward N. Jones, state director of the Works Progress Administration. In the next two years, the two men succeeded in getting President Franklin Roosevelt enthusiastic about the project. Studies done on the old South Penn indicated that its tunnels were still in amazingly good shape and that the workmanship was of high quality. Only three miles of total tunnel length remained to be completed. In January 1937, the Pennsylvania Turnpike Commission was created at the recommendation of the state legislature and signed into law on May 21, 1937. With Roosevelt's clout behind the project, federal funding was assured. Thousands of new jobs were created as work got underway. Three years later in October, 1940, America's first superhighway became a reality. "Nobody had ever seen a road without stoplights, intersections, steep hills and sharp curves," according to Harry Lundy, one of the turnpike's engineers. "That first Sunday it opened it was so crowded they couldn't get off at the interchanges." Motorists

lined up for ten hours before the Turnpike opened just for the novelty of taking a ride. William H. Shank has written a fascinating history of the Turnpike called *Vanderbilt's Folly, from* which this information comes.

Today, the Pennsylvania Turnpike extends from Philadelphia west to Youngstown, Ohio, and from Philadelphia east to Scranton. Few highways in America are crowded with as many tractor trailers hauling freight across the land. In fact, Pennsylvania's economy relies so heavily on trucks that the state produces the most tractor trailer bodies in America. The motorist who stops to nap in his car at any one of dozens of Pennsylvania truck stops will find himself surrounded by enormous trucks. Their drivers may be inside the restaurant eating a huge meal, or in the motel sleeping, but the engines of their trucks will still be idling. To wake up in a parking lot in the middle of the night surrounded by such rumbling mastodons is an experience one never forgets. Yet ever mindful of the important roll they play in our daily lives.

The same is true of a great many other experiences and recorded images about this great state, for the list seems endless.

Nearly 300 years have passed since William Penn sailed up the Delaware River. His legacy, the state of Pennsylvania born in 1774, is now over 200 years old. In many places its natural beauty is as wild and lovely as it must have been when Penn arrived.

But the true test of any settled region is whether it has been improved or spoiled by the presence of man. Perhaps because Pennsylvania is so large, one tends to overlook the places where industry and mineral exploitation have scarred the land. What one remembers best are the villages, towns, and entire regions where generations of settlers have continually upgraded the environment in ways which few places in America can match.

The enlightened Quaker principles of spiritual and political liberty which William Penn brought with him to the New World are still reflected in the Pennsylvania of today.

USS Olympia anchored at Penns Landing, Philadelphia. It was Admiral Dewey's flagship at the Battle of Manila Bay, on May 1, 1898.

Frost covered weeds prove exciting when viewed at close range. Right: Lighthouse on Presque Isle, a sandy peninsula washed by waters of Lake Erie. It is temporarily blanketed with winter's generous gift.

Trout fisherman tries his
skill on Oil Creek near Titusville. This northwestern
Pennsylvania town is site of
this nation's first oil well
completed August 28, 1859.
Left: Blazing autumn foliage
in Allegheny National Forest.
It encompasses an area of
over 500,000 acres.

Amish lady hustles to her
waiting buggy on a rainy
autumn day near Christiana.
Right: The broad Delaware
River separates Pennsylvania
from New York state near the
town of Shohola. Pages 40
and 41 following: Winter sky
forewarns of an approaching
storm over Amish farms at
New Holland.

The wind howls and temperature drops to well below zero during a blizzard which all but obliterates a farm near Somerset. Right: Frosty trees in Slippery Rock Creek Gorge near New Castle. Pages 44 and 45 following: "Amber waves of grain . . ." Fields of oats and spacious countryside near Lavansville.

Misty morning sunrise at Lake Jean, Ricketts Glen State Park. Left: Breathtaking orchid display at Longwood Gardens Horticultural Conservatory, Kennett Square. One of the most extensive botanical gardens in the United States.

The wild Youghiogheny River plunges through a breathtaking gorge in Ohiopyle State Park where white water enthusiasts enjoy some of Pennsylvania's best rapids, thrills, and often spills, galore. Right: Buildings erected in Philadelphia near turn of century, offer change of pace, when compared with present trends in design.

Thousands of flowering dogwood trees blanket Valley Forge National Park in early spring. Right: Huntsman and Whip lead a pack of hounds on a fox hunt at Doe Run.

Furious storm rams the shore of Lake Erie at dusk depositing chunks of ice that build up mountainous dunes. Right: Slippery Rock Creek at McConnells Mill State Park.

A young buck wallows in deep snow along the shore of Lake Erie at Presque Isle State Park. Right: Mid-winter snow storm enhances the beauty of Town Hall in Carlisle. Pages 56 and 57 following: British troops advance at Brandywine battle re-enactment.

George Washington statue at his Valley Forge Headquarters. Building in background was occupied during the winter of 1777-78. Left: Roblen purebred Cheviot sheep farm near Warrensville. Pages 60 and 61 following: Windblown grass tassels reflect a substantial growth pattern on farm, near Valley Forge.

Longwood Gardens Horticultural Conservatory at Kennett Square. It houses spectacular year-round shows of flowers and tropical plants. Right: Perfectly preserved round barn near the village of Old Fort.

Duquesne Incline, erected in 1877, rises up precipitous bluffs of Mt. Washington in Pittsburgh. Cable drum and wooden-toothed drive gear, part of original installation, are still in use. Left: Frigid winter day near Washington. A reluctant peek at the thermometer revealed 15 degrees below zero.

Elegant stairway inside the State Capitol Building at Harrisburg, established in 1812. Right: Pennsylvania state flag flies above Capitol Building. The architecture was influenced by St. Peter's Basilica in Rome.

Sunlight and shadows high-
light farm and village church
at White Pine. Left: Mennonite lass waves a friendly
"hello" as mother loads
groceries into the family
buggy at a shopping center
in Mifflinburg.

Misty morning on the Allegheny River near Kinzua Dam, Warren. Right: Joggers may tally up the trees as they lope along path in Fairmount Park, Philadelphia. Pages 72 and 73 following: Panoramic view of Philadelphia from Fairmount Park reveals setting sun in window reflections.

Union troops engage in battle re-enactment of Pickett's charge at Gettysburg. The casualties suffered here broke the back of Lee's army. Left: Square Rigger anchored at Penns Landing on the Delaware River, Philadelphia. Penn first set foot in his colony October 28, 1682. Pages 76 and 77 following: Confederate troops advance and fire on Union soldiers in Pickett's Charge battle re-enactment, Gettysburg.

A white on white snowscape reveals Welsh Hill Church on the fringe of Pennsylvania's Endless Mountains near Lenoxville. Right: White tail deer forage in deep snow at Presque Isle State Park in Lake Erie.

Friendly sow munches her dinner at a farm near Breeze-wood. Left: Fresh blanket of snow graces a homestead and gives definition to an open brook, on the outer perimeter of Pavia.

One room school house
in Amish country near
Bartville. Right: Blossoms of
apples and flowering crab
merge in colorful tapestry
at South Sterling.

Elfreth's Alley, in Philadelphia, dates back to the 1690's. The oldest continually occupied residential street in the nation. Left: Tattered original flag from Battle at Bull Run passes through the streets of Gettysburg during Independence Day parade.

Early fall foliage surrounds Baptist Church at Draper in Tioga County. Right: Brilliant autumn maples near Cogan House, along Pennsylvania Route 184. Pages 88 and 89 following: A rowing team and shell on the Schuylkill River, Philadelphia.

Colorful maple leaves cling tenaciously in early morning light at Prince Gallitzin State Park. Left: Silver Thread Falls in the Pocono Mountains near Dingmans Ferry. Pages 92 and 93 following: The Allegheny and Monongahela Rivers merge to form the Ohio River at Pittsburgh's famous Golden Triangle. Viewed from a bluff on Mt. Washington.

Stone barn near East Brad-
ford. Right: Gentle flowing
Pine Creek, near the village
of Cedar Run.

94

Flock of wild turkeys move cautiously through a dark forest in the Loyalsock River Valley. Left: Kinzua Bridge in the Seneca Highlands, an incredible feat of railroad engineering, is 2,053 feet long and 301 feet above the valley floor. It is believed to be the second highest viaduct on the North American continent.

A crowing rooster is framed
in a barn doorway at the
village of Millbach Springs.
Right: Pine Creek twists its
way through Pennsylvania's
Grand Canyon. View from
Leonard Harrison State Park
overlook.

Mushroom farm in abandoned limestone mine near Worthington, requires delicate attention. Mushrooms are harvested 365 days out of the year, leading all 50 states in the production of this edible growth. Left: One of 30 plus waterfalls formed by Kitchen Creek as it flows through Ricketts Glen State Park.

Ice storm in the Endless Mountain region glazes every limb and twig. Extreme close up reveals air bubbles in frozen drop hanging from a fir tree. Right: Elegant tulips embellish the appearance of County Municipal Building, Warren. Pages 104 and 105 following: Mountain laurel blossoms at the summit of 3,213 foot Mt. Davis, highest point in the state.

Amish farmer directs his team and harrow with attentive precision in field of young tobacco plants. Left: Budding grapevines in vineyard country neighboring the village of North East, close to shore of Lake Erie. Pages 108 and 109 following: Sailboat regatta reflects on calm waters of the Schuylkill River, Philadelphia.

Purple violets grow profusely along the Appalachian Trail near the Lehigh Valley. The famous Maine to Georgia trail passes through a long section of Pennsylvania on its more than 2,000 mile length. Right: Monument at Valley Forge. Here Washington endured his darkest moments of the Revolution during the winter of 1777-78.

Gettysburg National Park where the most decisive battle of the Civil War was fought in 1863. The terrible war raged for two more years, but Gettysburg was the turning point for the Confederacy. Right: Branches ladened with ice drape over Slippery Rock Creek at McConnells Mill State Park.

Covered bridge spans Slippery Rock Creek at McConnells Mill State Park near New Castle. Left: A wall of giant icicles descend from a cliff in the Allegheny National Forest.

November freeze coats rocks at the site of an old mill in the community of Paradise. Right: Mist clings in the deep gorge of the Youghiogheny River near Ohiopyle State Park.

Mare and foal in spring pasture near Buell Corners. Left: Petersburg Toll House on this country's first National Road at Addison. Although construction did not start until 1811, the road's early beginnings trace back to the French and Indian war era. Pages 120 and 121 following: A vibrant sunset bathes the Pocono Mountains identified with forested valleys and rich limestone soils.

Raging waves and flying spray encrusts shoreline trees along Lake Erie during a bitter winter day. Right: Sweeping panorama across the rolling hills of Bedford county. Pages 124 and 125 following: An autumn sunrise bursts upon High Knob at World's End State Park.

Pine loaded with a muffin of snow at Presque Isle State Park. The park is a 3,200 acre peninsula jutting seven miles into Lake Erie. Left: A surprise late spring snowfall blankets a beech forest in the Pocono Mountains near Tobyanna.

Covered bridge near Bartville. These picturesque spans still ford streams along many rural roads. Right: Fall foliage blazes in this aerial view of Wellsboro. Pages 136 and 137 following: Ohiopyle Falls on the Youghiogheny River is the site of Pennsylvania's largest state park which rambles over 18,643 acres of the Laurel Highlands. It was here that George Washington, seeking a water route to Fort Pitt, now Pittsburgh, abandoned his hopes upon reaching the great falls at Ohiopyle.

Tug passes under Benjamin Franklin Bridge on the Delaware River at Philadelphia. Left: Flowering crab graces the grounds near Phipps Conservatory in Pittsburgh. Pages 140 and 141 following: A windy spring day generates ripples on a farm pond near McKnightstown.

Independence Hall, Philadelphia. It was here the Declaration of Independence was adopted and the Constitution written. Right: Stalactites come down and stalagmites rise upward as they merge into beautiful formations at Penns Cave, Centre Hall.

Azalea blossoms spread a colorful array along the residential streets of Center Square. Left: Two little Amish girls return home from school with their brightly colored lunch boxes and snuggly mufflers. One girl walks backward to avoid being photographed.

Crown vetch at Hopewell Village National Historic Site. Right: Oil Creek and farmland south of Spartansburg.

Aerial view of Canada geese
in flight across Tioga county.
Left: Dingman's Falls in the
Delaware River Valley of the
Pocono Mountains.

A dusting of snow brightens a landscape near Breezewood. Right: Flowering tree in the Delaware River Valley heralds the first sign of spring. Pages 152 and 153 following: Summer clouds drift lazily over broad valley near Hazleton, where anthracite coal and the emergence of the railroad age shaped the area's destiny for many years.

Stony Fork creek cascades over rocky ravine at Draper. Left: Strasburg Railroad passes through the very heart of Lancaster County's Old Order Amish country. Pages 156 and 157 following: The monument at Gettysburg National Military Park, honors the sons of Pennsylvania who fought and died in our tragic Civil War. It is the largest battlefield shrine in America, with over 1,000 monuments and cannons along 35 miles of scenic avenues.

Philadelphia's towering City Hall is seen faintly through the gushing fountains at Logan Circle on the Benjamin Franklin Parkway. Right: Farm near Somerset, situated in a region that was originally a hunting ground for the Delaware, Shawnee and Iroquois Indians.

Immaculate farms flourish
throughout the state. This
one is no exception near
Doylestown. Left: Slender
sycamores along the banks
of Little Pine Creek,
Carsontown.

Daniel Boone homestead near Reading; birthplace of America's great frontiersman. Right: Wild Canada goose prepares to land on the Schuylkill River.

Lacy veils spill over a ledge along Falls Trail at Ricketts Glen State Park. Right: Covered bridge spans Brush Creek near Breezewood. Pages 168 and 169 following: Canada geese feed along Schuylkill River, Philadelphia. They are wary and intelligent birds reaching an age of 20 years or more.

Corn cribs reveal a bountiful harvest at Penns Creek. Right: A cock ring neck pheasant struts in a meadow along the Loyalsock River. It is one of Pennsylvania's chief game birds. Pages 172 and 173 following: Chilly autumn nights generate fog in the valley floors of the state's highlands. This early morning view of the Loyalsock Valley is from High Knob near Worlds End State Park.

Foliage basks in the dazzling sunlight of a hardwood forest. Right: A red ball of fire rises seemingly from the water at Prince Gallitzin State Park.

Gleaming white restored buildings at Hopewell Village National Historic Site. It is a reconstructed iron-making village near Morgan-town. Left. The clip-clop of horses hooves resound throughout the Amish coun-tryside. Steam belches from this steed on a cold day in the community of Intercourse.

Fairmount Park in Philadelphia has the distinction of being the largest city park in the world. Some of Philadelphia's greatest historic and cultural treasures lie within its 8,000 acres, including handsome sculpture as shown of Fredrick Remington's, "Cowboy". Right: The golden light of an autumn morning illuminates ferns in Pennsylvania's Laurel Highlands.

Blazing sky at sunset silhouettes a scrub pine along the Laurel Ridge Trail. Right: Two bumble bees crowd on a thistle while a sulphur butterfly flits overhead.

Windswept countryside near Lavansville. Left: A 37 foot statue of William Penn, the founder of Pennsylvania, tops the unusual tower structure of Philadelphia's famous City Hall. A showplace of history, architecture, art and craftsmanship from a former age. Pages 184 and 185 following: Cross country skier on the Appalachian Trail at Delaware Water Gap. Below sheer cliffs, the frozen river twists through a narrow defile that separates Pennsylvania from New Jersey.

A curious buck at Nemacolin Park near Farmington. Right: An Amish elder peers from his buggy while his stately steed awaits his master's command to proceed. Pages 188 and 189 following: Billowing clouds pass over a farm near Shelmadine Springs.

Tulips exemplify the refreshing beauty of spring near Doylestown. Right: Evening reflections on the Susquehanna River at Harrisburg.